DUE DATE **BRODART**		05/94	13.50
OCT 26 1998			

FUN
No Fun

by James Stevenson

Greenwillow Books, New York

Watercolor paintings were used
for the full-color art.
The text type is ITC Bookman.

Printed in Hong Kong by
South China Printing Company (1988) Ltd.

First Edition
10 9 8 7 6 5 4 3 2 1

Library of Congress
Cataloging-in-Publication Data
Stevenson, James (date)
Fun / no fun / by James Stevenson.
        p.   cm.
Summary:
The author recalls events in his childhood
and divides them into two important categories.
ISBN 0-688-11673-6 (trade).
ISBN 0-688-11674-4 (lib. bdg.)
1. Stevenson, James (date) — Biography—
Youth — Juvenile literature.
2. Authors, American —20th century—
Biography — Juvenile literature.
3. Illustrators — United States — Biography—
Juvenile literature.
[1. Stevenson, James (date).
2. Authors, American.   3. Illustrators.]
I. Title.   PS3569.T455Z473   1994
813'.54—dc20   [B]
93-18187   CIP   AC

When I was young (a long time ago),
some things were fun,
and some things were no fun.

FUN

NO FUN

cowboy boots

galoshes

baseball hat

cap with flaps

cookies with raisins

cookies with no raisins

ice skates

roller skates

FUN

NO FUN

water pistols

dominoes

listening to "The Shadow"
on the radio

listening to Mr. Carnes
at school

seeing an eclipse
of the moon

BUT I'M
NOT TIRED!

I'LL GO TO BED
EARLY FOR A
WHOLE WEEK!

NO

I'LL SLEEP LATE
TOMORROW!

NO

BILLY FOSTER
IS ALLOWED!

I NEVER
SEE IT!

NO

I'LL JUST
LIE AWAKE
ANYWAY!

not being allowed
to stay up
until midnight
on New Year's Eve

The village was fun:

In the grocery
Mr. Finn used
a long stick
with pincers
to get boxes down
from the high shelves.

The cleaner's was
always full of steam.

CLICKETY
CLACKETY

The five-and-ten had small wires
along the ceiling. Small boxes
went rattling around the store
to where people made change.

The newspaper office
thundered and shook and clattered,
and it smelled of ink.

When they washed the fire engine
at the firehouse, the street
filled with soapy water.

Fun was sitting on the porch
with my father and Jocko,
watching a thunderstorm coming.

No fun was when the storm arrived
and the lightning crashed.

Fun was going into the marsh where the skunk cabbage grew,

scooping up
a handful of mud,

wrapping the mud in the
skunk cabbage leaf,

picking a leaf
of skunk cabbage,

making it just right…

and throwing it at your friends.

No fun was going home afterward.

Some dogs were fun, and some weren't.

Our dog,
Jocko, was fun —
when he was awake.

The Hoppers' —
never.

My friend Larry's —
always.

Mrs. DeSalvo's —
hardly ever.

Mr. Kellogg's —
I never got close enough to find out.

Fun was being a Cub Scout.

No fun was going to a Cub Scout
meeting if you had to walk
past tough kids to get there.

Fun was after we raked up
all the leaves,
when my friends and I
could jump in the pile.

Fun was later,
when my father burned
the pile of leaves.
A wonderful smell
filled the neighborhood.

Fun was when we went to pay a call
on Miss Van Cortlandt. She was over
100 years old, and her house was
supposed to have a ghost in it.

Not quite so much fun
was when she showed me
the ghost room.
It was dark and creepy.

Fun was racing around our cellar
on a sled that had wheels.

Fun was when we begged our
mother to sing "Rock of Ages,"
and she did. (She couldn't
carry a tune.)

Driving to Bear Mountain
was fun and no fun and fun again.

FUN

my birthday

Christmas

Fourth of July

Thanksgiving (the food part)

Valentine's Day (sometimes)

April Fool's Day

NO FUN

New Year's Day

Labor Day

Valentine's Day (sometimes)

my brother's birthday

No fun was when my parents
went on a trip without me.

Fun
was getting ready to put on a play
in our cellar.

No fun

was the play itself.

Fun was when
the ice cream truck came.

No fun was when
you had no money.

No fun
was trying to teach Jocko tricks.

Fun
was getting a violin
on my birthday.
It came in
a green case.

No fun

was practicing the violin

or the lessons with Mrs. Mullen.

Fun
was when we got ice cream
for lunch at school.
They were called
"Dixie cups."

We pulled off
the tops,

and there was a picture
of a movie star
we had never seen.

"WHO DID YOU GET?"
"RAMON NAVARRO."
"I'LL TRADE YOU FOR
A TOM MIX."

 Then we ate the ice cream.

Fun was when our friend Tony
took a cookie,

poked a hole
in it,

and pretended to be
an Englishman
with a monocle.

Fun was when the teacher was busy.

Fun was
getting everybody
into the booth at the
same time for a picture,

then seeing the photos.

OOH!
LOOK AT ME!

HIDEOUS!

THAT ONE'S
GOOD OF
YOU

Fun was going to the amusement park.

No fun
was when I discovered
it was too late
to change my mind
about going on a ride.

No fun was having to go home
without seeing the really good stuff.

But the most fun
of all was going to the woods…

and making a dam in the stream.

At the end of the day, fun was going to sleep
thinking about what fun it would be tomorrow.

Sometimes it still is.